Egyptian Mythology Illustrated for Beginners.

"Do not separate your heart from the tongue, and all your actions will be successful."
(Amenmope)

Summary:

CONTENTS:

Mythology is an integral part of human civilization, and in Greek mythology, in particular, Western culture has its roots, so much so that artists and thinkers continue to read the condition and events of contemporary man against the backdrop of Greek myth. From the eighteenth century onwards this immense patrimony has been the subject of an organic scientific discipline, which is intertwined with the study of anthropology, ethnography, psychoanalysis, literature, art, philosophy. In this volume a clear, concise and rigorous introduction to the knowledge of Greek mythology is presented. Starting from the possible definitions of the myth, the work proposes a typology of myths exposed in a simple way for everyone, then illustrating the interpretations developed by the Greeks themselves.

Chapter 1

CREATION FOR THE ANCIENT EGYPTIANS

Tales of Egyptian gods are thousands of years old. Archaeologists, who collect artifacts and documents of antiquity, trace the first traces of the Egyptians to about five thousand years before Christ.

So, when have the legends about gods been around? They have been handed down to us through engraved stones, paintings, papyri and the stories of Greek travellers. However, some scholars argue that they were already told, without being written, long before the invasion of the hieroglyphs, that is about three thousand years before Christ.

THE STARRY SKY OF EGYPT

Undoubtedly, the sky of ancient Egypt was that of today. Under the African sun, from north to south, the territory of ancient Egypt stretched from the Mediterranean sea to the great deserts of Sudan, like today.

Here the Nile transforms the sand of its fertile land banks. It marked the division of the territory into two parts: Lower Egypt, near the source and Upper Egypt, at the mouth.

The great cities, Heliopolis, Memphis, Ermopoli, Thebes, each had their own divinities. When wars were fought between different cities, the victors imposed their deities on the vanquished. Over the centuries, the distinction between local divinities and "adopted" divinities has been lost, the gods were everyone's patrimony.

There were thousands of names of different deities, hundreds of temples, treasures galore, endless stories. The first told speak of the beginning of time, of the creation of the world.

THE SUN GOD

The legend that comes from Heliopolis begins like this: before creation, the sea flooded everything. It came out of nowhere, without movement, nor noise, nor lapping: the immense body of the god Nu, the Ocean.

How many days did it take to cover the earth? Nobody knows. Time also did not exist.

It is the beginning and a fundamental event is anticipated. From the most remote depths, with all its grandeur, here is a mountain emerging from the waters. A red sun shines on its top. Nace Atum, the sun god.

In Egyptian mythology, Atum-Sun has a face, two arms and two legs; in short, he has the appearance of a man. His energy is that of the universe, it contains all the other divinities and all the forces of the earth, both the good ones and the destructive ones.

His first act is to become a

father. It is not known with certainty how it happened; some argue that atum, as soon as he appeared, generated his same semen Shu, male divinity, and Tefnut, female divinity, his twin. Others claim that both originated from his throat: Shu from a spit and Tefnut from a cough.

This hypothesis is supported by the fact that shu means "air" or "void" and tefnut means "imidity" or "rigiada".

Shu and Tefnut are brother and sister, but also lovers and they come together to create the goddess Nut, the Sky, and the god Geb, the land of Egypt. Geb extends over his kingdom, the earth; Nut, arches over Geb and pushes Nu.Oceano behind him, which becomes a lake; this event irritates the god, forced to make some room for his descendants.

THE AIR, THE SKY, THE EARTH

At this point, all the forces of the universe have been created, the sun, the air, the sky, the earth. Atum is satisfied and casting a glance on his creation, he orders Shu, god of Air, to separate Nut-Heaven from Geb-Earth.

Shu-Aria, a divinity often represented in Egyptian paintings with a head adorned with an ostrich feather, obeys: he raises her arm to remove her daughter-Heaven, the beautiful Nut, from the body of Geb, her brother and husband. .

This is why the sky will forever be above our heads, the earth under our feet and the air between heaven and earth.

However, in the Egyptian drawings, Nut is always depicted while observing Geb;

the two are also joined with thin hands and light feet. In Egypt, between heaven and between there is a great love story.

THE OTHER LEGENDS

Another legend tells of the creation of the world: as the mountain emerges from the water, a lotus flower blooms.

Crouching inside the flower, Atum appears with the appearance of a small, shining child. When the flower closes, it hides the child-light; the next morning it opens and makes it visible.

The child-god created the world; the other gods came out of his mouth and men out of his eyes. In Egypt, in fact, the word that means "men" and the one that means "tears" have the same pronunciation.

In other legends, it is Thoth, the god of Wisdom, who starts the world. On the island born from the earthquake of the waters of Nu, eight divinities have taken the form of frogs or snakes.

They created the sun from an egg that Thoth, the god with the head of an ibis (a bird with a long curved beak), brought to the top of the mountain. Having accomplished their task, the eight divinities withdrew; then Thoth began the construction of the temple in honor of the sun god, Ra.

And where the egg hatched, where fragments of the shell remained, the capital of the land of Egypt had to be built. In Menfi this legend was told: on the mountain that emerged for the first time from the waters of Nu the wise god Ptah appeared

magnanimous and very intelligent, he has the great

power to evoke an image and give it life by giving it a name: from him were born the other divinities and all living beings. The moment he receives the name, each being also receives life.

Ptah is not content with animating everything by naming it, but he also invents cities and temples; than he invented the production of bread and teaches it to the inhabitants of the earth, men. In Thebes, another story was circulating: an unknown deity, perhaps the wind god Amun, whose name means "hidden", blew on the surface of the ancestor of the gods, the ocean Nu, an immense lifeless being. And after blowing, he let out the cry of the goose, intelligent bird.

At the echo of that cry, Amon took the shape of the sun that shines in the sky. Later, the mystery Amon intervened in the life of the kings of Egypt, the pharaohs.

He, the invisible god, took on the guise of the ruling pharaoh and took his place next to the queen. The latter, without recognizing the god (who could? No one has ever seen him) conceived a child with them. Not just any child, but the future pharaoh Amehotep III.

He is associated with a ka, the source of eternal life, which is born with the pharaoh and allows him to become immortal.

THE IDEA OF MEN

Who came up with the idea of creating men? A strange deity, honored in the Nile caves of Other Egypt, Khnum, the ram-headed god. With great patience and wisdom, he built little men out of clay, very well made.

He knew which organs to put inside the body, he knew the place of the heart, the attachment points of the bones and the path of the veins. He created strong and intelligent men with dark skin; since he was in charge of looking after future generations, he had to guarantee a good offspring, indispensable for the welfare of the gods who fed on offerings.

THE PERFECT ORDER

Men began to build temples and to celebrate the cult of the sun god to thank him and ask him to maintain harmony in the world as at the time of creation.

No doubt, if anything changed in the early days of their civilization, there would be serious problems. This is the opinion of Atum-Ra, who wisely guides the other deities behind the great father Nu, who has calmed down completely and transformed what remains of his primeval celestial waters into a magnificent great river, the Nile, and into benefactor rains.

For a certain period, all creation remained perfect. The gods were quiet and lived in peace. To tell the truth, not everything was calm.

Nut, the goddess of Heaven always maintains her achromatic position above Geb, god of the Earth, but during the night she stretches out towards him. Geb, approaches and kisses her.

They are therefore lovers; even if it is strange, among gods of the Egyptians it often happens that brothers and sisters are spouses or lovers. Geb and Nut meet without the knowledge of their grandfather, Atum-Sole.

These have other concerns. Men in temples are not always devoted and sometimes forget to thank Atum, the creator of the universe.

THE CHILDREN OF HEAVEN

Following their secret loves, Nut becomes pregnant with her husband Geb. She is not of a single child, but of couple! As soon as he hears the news,

Atum goes on a rampage. Since he is a god, he makes an extraordinary decision: he prevents nut from giving birth! Nut is desperate.

How to bear a desperate sky? All the other deities would like to help her, but it is impossible: the power of atum is absolute. But the order is so absurd that it irritates Thoth, the god of Wisdom.

Let us remember that Thoth, who came from another legend, is the god with the ibis temptation; and with his great intelligence he has already thought of a solution for this case. Atum forbade Nut to give birth.

The prohibition concerns the time created by Atum himself, which is counted in years of three hundred and sixty days and three hundred and sixty nights.

THOT'S SOLUTION

Thoth, who has the head of an ibis but the arms and legs of a man, approaches the Moon and offers her to play dice. The game promises to be exciting and Lunta has a lot of time.

The problem is precisely this: time.

Thot proposes to the Moon to earn fear. The winner of the game will get no money, but seconds, minutes, hours, and why not, days.

The Moon accepts: it is a lot of fun to play in the firmament of the sky with an intelligent opponent. They are two good players and they keep rolling the dice, never stopping. Nut is very worried about her children who are asking to be born.

Eventually Thot returns triumphant: he has not only gained many minutes and a few hours, but even five full days, five times twenty-four hours, to be used immediately, while the news has not leaked yet. Nut can therefore give birth without disobeying the sun god.

In fact the power of Atum is not valid these days, as they were not created by him. Thor can really be proud of the idea of him. The Egyptians, on the other hand, will always remain a little indifferent at the end of the year; these are days when anything can happen.

THE FIVE COME FROM HEAVEN

Each child has his or her day of birth.

The first is a male, Osiris, handsome, sweet-eyed, with olive skin and broad shoulders. It is already said that he will be righteous, strong and good.

He is the primogent and the heir of his father Geb, the earth, which gives him the power to reign over Egypt. Osiris will be the first pharaoh.

A second son is born the next

day, Horus, the Ancient.

This son has the head of a hawk and will be feared by all other deities. He is the god of war. On the third day Nut would like to repossess in an oasis but here comes out of her body, no one knows how, wounding her, the violent Seth, the red god with two horns, god of lightning, deserts, revenge, jealous god, combative , cheater, the traitor of history. We will also see that he will know how to be devoted and courageous. Not always everything is negative.

Nu, without knowing

precisely what really happened, gives birth to the first child after four days in a reed bed. She is the graceful and harmonious Isis with magnificent hair, a very good and intelligent sorceress, without equal.

On the fifth day, to these four phenomena, her sister Nephthys adds, sweet, so sweet that no one would know how to contradict her, even when she becomes the mother of Anubis, god with the head of a jackal, and aunt of little Horus ... but this is a ' another story.

CHAPTER 2

LOCAL DEITIES OF ANCIENT EGYPT

The Egyptians were polytheists, like all peoples of antiquity, except

of the Jews first and of the Christians and Muslims then.

They worshiped many divinities (even 700), each of which had its priests, its temples, its lands:

The priests of a god had, among others, the task of administering its goods and naturally benefited from it.

The Egyptians worshiped any object or being that they considered useful or dangerous.

Among the animals (zoolatry) the ox called Apis was worshiped, very useful for all jobs,

the cow, the cat exterminating the mice that infested Egypt, the monkey, the hippo,

the scorpion, the lion, the snake and the crocodile.

The cult of animals was always present among the Egyptians despite the transition from hunting to agriculture.

Some sacred animals were kept in temples as living representations of deities.

When these animals died they

were mummified and buried in special tombs.

Mummified animals of many species have been found: from crocodiles, to cats, to ibises.

It was believed that a

mummified animal could carry messages and prayers to the deity.

This conception enabled many temples to derive a source of income from it.

The hawk, which the Egyptians saw flying high in the sky and observing the earth with its sharp eyes

for these characteristics it became a natural symbol of the sun.

and when, starting from the 4th dynasty, the pharaoh began to call himself "Son of Ra",

the falcon, symbol of Horus and Ra became a way to

identify the pharaoh.

Falcons and falcon-winged sun discs decorate almost all temples in Egypt.

The snake, and in particular the

female cobra, was the symbol of the goddess Wadjet (Uadjet).

which means "The Green", "That of the color of the papyrus",

who protected the flood necessary for the survival of the country, and for this she became the protector of Lower Egypt,

In this capacity, the image of the female snake was placed on the forehead of the pharaoh,

the one who represented the solar god Ra on earth.

So the snake on the crown of the ruler symbolizes the destructive force, in the service

of the ruler
to exterminate his enemies,
who are also Egypt's enemies.

The cobra protected the pharaoh (and the sun) by spitting poison at his enemies.

Wadjet was therefore a kind of "good snake", who watched so that the world did not fall into chaos.

In general, however, snakes were mostly seen as dangerous animals, regardless of the fact whether the species they belonged to was poisonous or not.

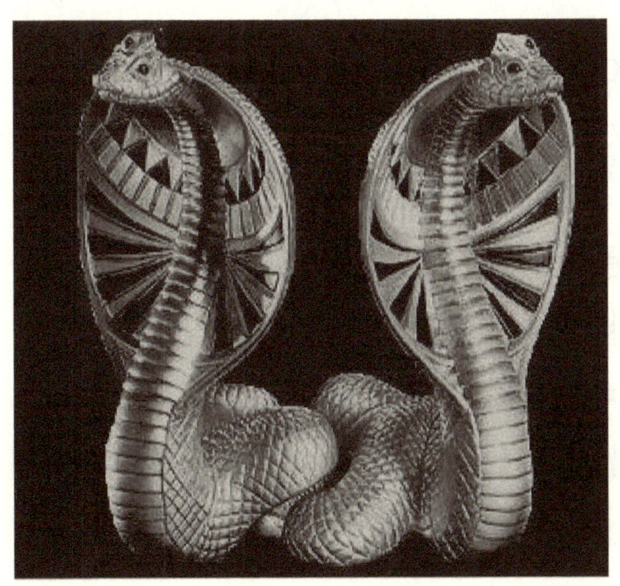

It was believed that the afterlife was full of snakes representing the power of chaos,

that threatened the smooth functioning of the world.

The main example of a "bad" snake was Apophis the great cosmic snake,

wrapped around the earth,

which continually threatened to destroy it.

The sun was in constant struggle with Apophis to try to defeat him and to restore order in the world.

In this fight, every night Apophis tried to swallow all the water in the sea

to surround the sun while he travelled on the boat that took it to the afterlife

and every night the deities who kept order in the world managed to get the better of him.

But this victory could not be taken for granted.

The cow represented the goddess Hathor who was the main deity of love and fertility, she also represented the goddess of beauty and music.

She was often represented with a woman with cow horns.

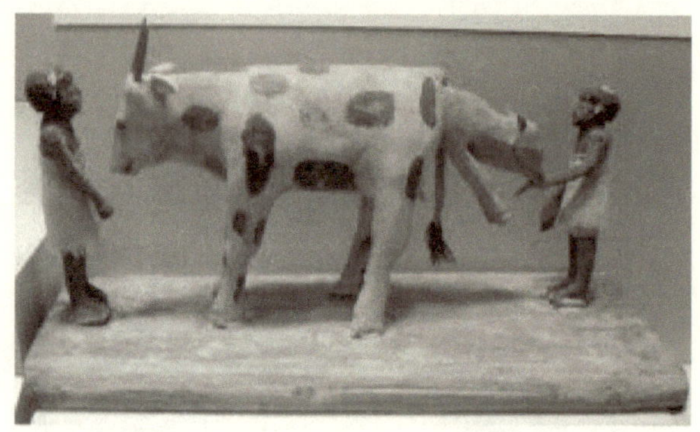

The baboon was associated with the moon deity Thoth, who was also the god of wisdom.

Many statuettes or amulets of the god show him as a seated baboon, often with his hands raised

and wearing a sun disk or a crescent moon in his hand.

The Egyptians thought that baboons, who used to sit with

their heads facing east

just before sunrise and waved their paws when they saw the sun rise,

were able to predict the sunrise and celebrated it.

The baboon thus became the symbol of the wisdom of the world

and as such he was considered the inventor of writing and the patron saint of scribes.

Perhaps to remember the industriousness of the fly, which never stands still,
the pharaoh gave as a prize gold amulets in the shape of a

fly,

to the soldiers who had fought with particular valor and self-denial in war.

The "Order of the Golden Fly" was awarded for particularly daring and courageous actions.

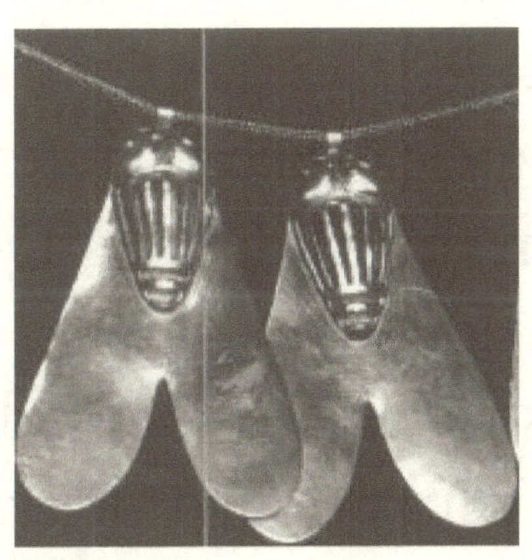

The cat, which for us is a pet, was originally a wild animal.

The Egyptians began to domesticate it among other things for his ability

to keep small rodents away from homes and food supplies.

A representation of the sun god Ra was "the big cat"

protector of the solar course from the dangers of the snake Aphopis.

Cats, and especially female cats, from the Middle Kingdom were considered

animals sacred to the goddess Bastet, a very popular deity,

daughter of Ra, who reigned over love, fertility and feast days.

Bastet was depicted as a cat or with the head of a cat and the body of a woman.

Sacred cats lived in the Bastet temple and were mummified when they died

dehydrating their bodies with

Natron, with a similar process to that used for human mummification.

They were then wrapped in a linen bandage, with the legs parallel to the body.

Their head was covered with a bronze mask with their effigy and the burial consisted of a sarcophagus in the shape of a seated cat, then placed in the temple cemetery.

Huge cemeteries containing thousands of burials of these animals have been discovered.

The main center for the worship of the goddess Bastet was the city of Tell Basta.

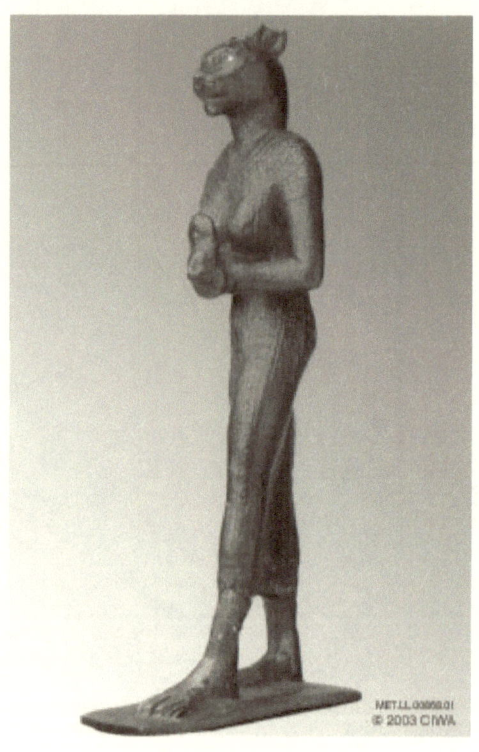

The scarab represented a form of the sun god Ra.

In nature, the beetle composes a ball of fresh dung in which it lays its eggs and then rolls it to a safe place.

When their young are born, they depend on dung as a source of nourishment.

The Egyptians, seeing the scarab come out of the ball of dung which he then pushed,

they believed that the insect created itself and could be compared to the god Ra

pushing the ball of the sun in front of him.

So the scarab was revered on the one hand as "Khepri", the one who comes out of the earth,

and on the other hand as Atum, demiurge god, self-created, origin of the gods and of the entire universe.

In fact, the Egyptians thought that both life and the order of the universe had originated from a state of chaos.

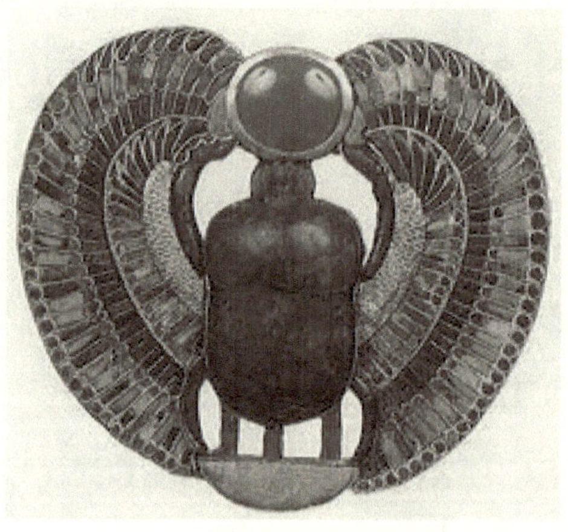

The panther was believed to have the power to protect the ruler.

She was revered because she was connected to the sun god

and the sky goddess.

It represented the night sky and, consequently, the Kingdom of the Underworld.

The ram with curved horns was one of the animals sacred to the sun god Amon-Ra,

but also to Khnum, a divinity that the Egyptians believed had been, with his potter's wheel,

the creator of all from the mud of the Nile.

A prayer dedicated to him reads as follows:

Oh Amon, Amon, who art in Heaven

Father of One who has no Mother.

How sweet it is to say your name.

Give us the joy of life, the taste of bread for the baby,

Your will be done on Earth as it is in Heaven.

You made me see the darkness, create the light for me.

Give me your grace, let me see you continuously!

In Egypt, religion was sharply divided between the official state cult

and cult practices of the mass of the population.

We are poorly informed about the latter, while we know divine worship very well,

which took place in temples all over Egypt and especially funerary cults,

thanks to the extraordinary amount of news

provided us by the myriads of tombs discovered by

archaeologists.

Each city was linked to different deities and, often, the deity of the city

who took over became the main deity

(at least as long as that city continued to hold power).

The great deities were represented both in anthropomorphic form (human form),

both in zoomorphic form (human body and animal head).

However, the religious experience of the Egyptians was concentrated

especially on the great

mystery of death and life in the afterlife.

For the Egyptians there was a divinity for every aspect of nature and life.

The most important god was Amon-Ra, the sun,

whose energy fertilizes the Earth; his name means who creates everything."

He was the son of Nun and Neith.

After Ra there was the Goddess Isis (the moon) who indicated the most suitable periods for sowing and harvesting.

She was the goddess of mothers, children and moon goddess, she became her, after bringing Osiris back to life, goddess of medicine.

She married and was the sister of Osiris and mother of the falcon-god Horus,

she was the daughter of Nut and Geb (read Enneade).

Isis has a throne-shaped headdress or horns on her head with a moon,

she is often represented with outstretched wings.

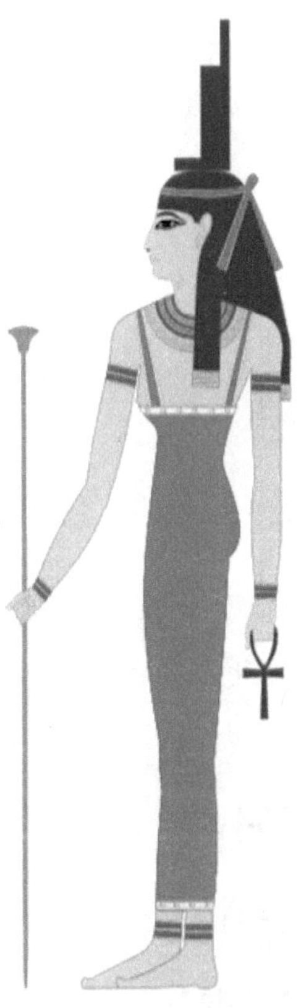

Then there was Osiris (read myth), brother and husband of Isis.

God of death and life and above all god of agriculture and vegetation.

He was killed and dismembered by his evil brother Seth and reassembled and brought back to life by Isis.

He was later embalmed by Anubis, thus going to reign in the world of the dead

The figure of him is linked to the rising sun and the fertilizing Nile.

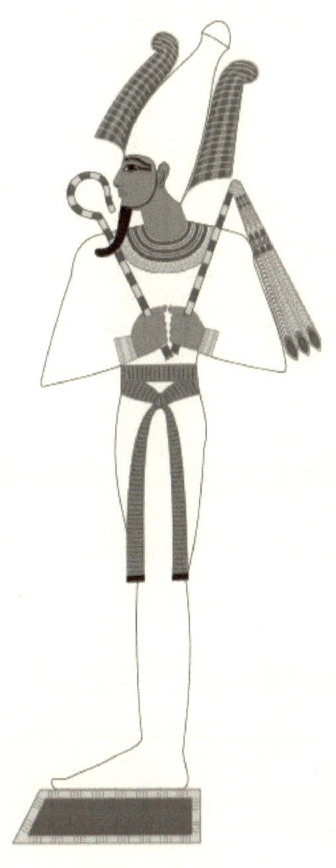

Atum was the lord of the deities who had created himself before generating Shu and Tefnut

and had his shadow as his

bride.

He originated from the "Nun", the primordial soup in which he already existed as a spirit,

but he became a reality only when Ptah uttered its name.

Atum is seen as a man sometimes seated on a throne, sometimes standing,

bearing on his head a crown with the symbols of Lower and Upper Egypt.

He believed himself to be the creator of the universe under the name of Atum-Ra.

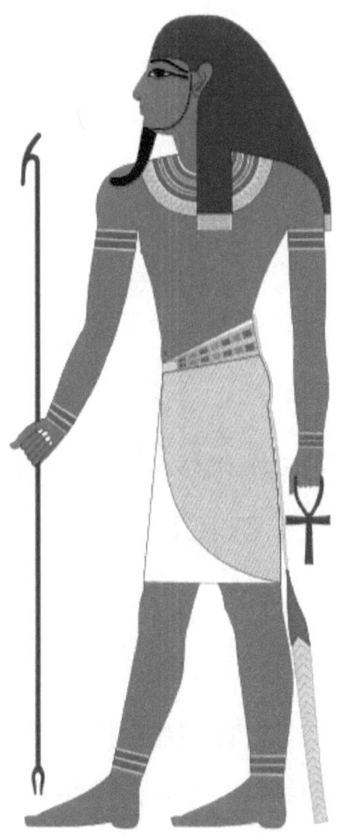

Jackal-headed Anubis was the God of the kingdom of the dead, judge of souls, and accompanied the transition from this to the other life.

He assisted Horus and Thoth in weighing the hearts of the dead

and he was the illegitimate son of Osiris and Nefthi

The goddess Qeb-hwt, also known as Kebechet

or " who pours fresh water" and who refreshed the dead, she was considered the daughter of Anubis and sometimes her sister.

Indicated in the ancient hieroglyphs, as "Young dog", it is also called Imy-ut: the embalmer.

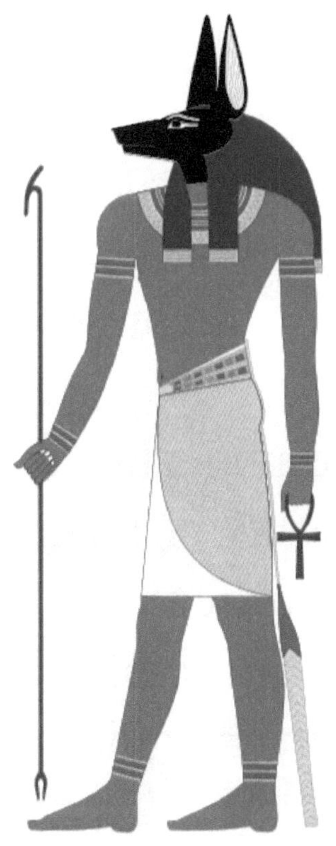

Hathor was Horus's wife-cow goddess and represented the sun.

Her name means "House of Horus" probably referring to

the myth according to which Horus,

identified as a celestial hawk-god and sun-god, at the end of his journey through the heavens,

in the evening he would return to Hathor's mouth to spend the night there, he

enjoyed a restful sleep and emerge again in the guise of the morning sun.

She was also defined: the "Great celestial cow that created the world and the sun."

and she was considered the patron goddess of love and the protector of music and dance.

A popular festival, that of "intoxication", was held every year in Denderah was the

main center of her cult, on the 20th day of the first month of the flood.

In addition, Hathor had the task of protecting the sources of the Nile,

Thoth, in Egyptian Djehuty, was the God of wisdom and wisdom,
inventor of writing and patron saint of scribes and

moon phases.

He is who kept track of everything that happened and who recorded the divine sentences.

He got from the Moon, five more days, to complete the year in 365 days.

The center of his cult was in Ermopoli, where he was considered the supreme god.

He was also the messenger of the gods and by the Greeks he was identified with Hermes

According to some he was the son of Ra, according to others he was born from the head of Seth.

Prayer of the scribes:

"O Thoth, keep me from empty words.

Stand behind me (to guide me) in the morning.

Come, you are the divine word.

You are a sweet source for the thirsty traveller in the desert ",

It is inaccessible to the talker, prodigal to the silent Seth, son of Geb, the earth (male principle) and Nut, the sky (female principle), brother of Osiris, Isis and Nephthys (of whom he was also the husband),

out of jealousy he organized a deadly conspiracy against his brother Osiris

who will then be avenged by the latter's son, Horus.

He was the Lord of the desert, adored by the caravans who moved from one oasis to another.

He was the god of war and brute force, which teaches subjugation

with the violent struggle to win in battle and find honor.

He represented the

indomitable forces of human nature and was the symbol of rebellion against the gods.

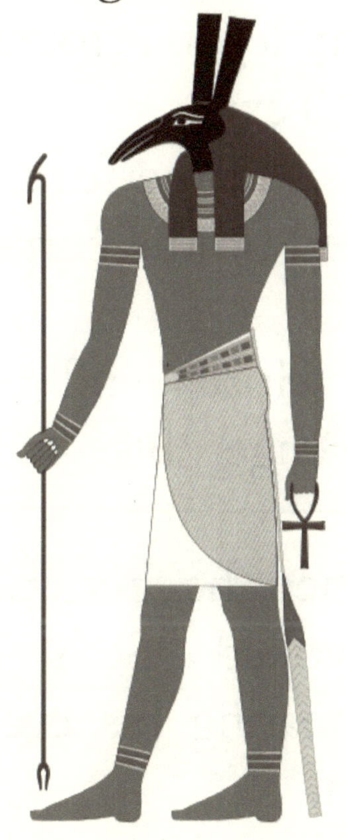

Horus, the falcon-god was the patron of the sky, god of light and goodness.

and above all god of the pharaoh,

An ancient legend found in the Pyramid Texts,

tells that Isis in the form of a vulture landed on the corpse of Osiris,

conceived Horus and raised him to avenge his father's death.

Horus, when he became an adult, provoked Seth who reacted by tearing his eye out during a fight,

but Horus took him back, won Seth and castrated him.

At this point the assembly of

the gods placed Horus on his father's throne.

Hence, he is the symbol of the winning power.

He was the husband of Hathor.

His eye is an amulet that destroys the wicked.

In fact, the myth of him tells that after defeating the evil god Seth,

Geb gave him a destructive amulet of wickedness.

He had four sons who gave their names to the canopic jars: Amset, Hapi, Duamutef and Qebehsenuf.

Amon is an Egyptian deity born from the fusion of the god Ra of Heliopolis
with the main Theban deity Amun

From what appears from the texts we possess, the merger was an agreement between the two priestly colleges

to ensure that the new deity was recognized as king of all the gods of the Egyptian pantheon.

The birth of Amon-Ra can be placed, during the historical phase called second intermediate period,

which includes the troubled story of the Hyksos domination.

The god was, in Thebes, husband of Mut and father of Khonsu, while in Heliopolis he was husband of Hathor and father of Harmachis

The most impressive temple of ancient Egypt was dedicated to Amon-Ra in Thebes,

the Great Temple of Amun

In the late stage of Egyptian history, when the office of Amun's first priest

became, in fact, the title of the one who ruled much of Egypt,

Amon-Ra rose to the rank of universal demiurge, creator of everything.

Amon was the solar God of Thebes whose name means "

who is hidden".

Together with his wife Mut and his son Khonsu he formed the triad of Thebes.

He was also the god of geese and curved-horned rams.

A shrine of him, dating back to the Middle Empire, is found in Karnak.

"Leaning before you stand the gods, praising the strength of the creator.

King and leader of every god, we celebrate your strength because you created us.

We worship you because you formed us.

We sing hymns of praise so that you protect us "

(Hymns of Amun).

Mut was the goddess of Thebes wife of the god Amun

Her name means "mother", of which she is therefore the protector.

She assumed particular importance in the New Kingdom, as the female counterpart of Ammon-Ra of Uaset (Thebes).

Together with him and Khons, she formed the Triad of Thebes.

She was also adored as a straightener of wrongs.

During the New Kingdom, the weddings of Mut and Amun were part of the great annual celebrations.

Once a year the procession of sacred boats came from Karnak across the river bearing the simulacrum of the three divinities, on the occasion of the feast of the opet.

After fourteen days of celebration, the boats returned to Karnak by land,

drag on rollers along a two-and-a-half kilometer avenue lined with ram-headed sphinxes.

Religiousness in Egypt was very strong and for this reason each village had its own patron god,

who was prayed and honored.

In the life of ancient Egypt, ordinary people did not normally go to the great temples.

In the house he had figurines of his favorite gods, one of them was that of the goddess Hator, goddess of dance and music

She participated in the processions for the most important ceremonies

of the great deities of the state, such as Amun and Osiris.

she preceded by the pharaoh,

the priests and the nobles.

These holidays were good occasions to celebrate.

While the men had houses of adobe and palm wood,

the abodes of the gods were made of stone because they had to be worthy of their inhabitants.

The oldest Egyptian temples were small, with non-permanent structures, but during the Ancient and Middle Kingdoms

their structures became more elaborate, and from this time they were built in stone.

According to this standard

plan, the temple was built along a central processional street

which led through a series of courtyards and halls to the sanctuary,

where a statue of the god of the temple was kept.

Access to this most sacred part of the temple was limited to the pharaoh and high-ranking priests.

The temples in fact were closed buildings, where the divinity "lived" in the form of a statue.

The choice of material did not derive only from the need to build solid and strong walls, but the stone, because of its consistency, was called the "material of eternity",

capable of bearing witness to the glory and power of the god throughout all time.

An avenue lined with statues of sphinxes, monsters with human heads on the body of a lion,

led to the monumental entrance, squeezed between two rectangular pillars.

Once past the pylons, the temple appeared.

There was a courtyard surrounded by a portico formed by one or two rows of columns.

The obelisks and columns were raised by force of arms

by a group of slaves pulling in various directions.

With this method, the correct position of the obelisks and columns could be guaranteed.

The obelisks and columns were richly decorated.

The people could only get here.

Then there was the reception room of the gods, a space with numerous large, narrow columns.

Only priests could enter this large room on feast days.

Beyond these columns the building squeezed, closing.
The light diminished and smaller and smaller doors led to magnificent halls with ceilings decorated with starry skies.
This series of rooms ended in the actual sanctuary,
where the statue of the divinity was placed, which was always covered with gold,
metal that represented the flesh of the gods.

In the temples the priests gathered and went to pray and worship the gods

or to teach children to read and write.

Pharaoh was the only man who was allowed to enter into relationship with the gods.

Only him, alone , could address them directly,

praying to them and asking for their blessing on Egypt.

However, the pharaoh delegated his religious power to a high priest,

with the task of some specific rites.

The temples were surrounded

by a large wall,

so that they were isolated from the world and therefore kept pure and sacred.

Before sunrise, there was a great movement in the kitchens of the temple, food was prepared for the Gods.

The priests, after having purified themselves with numerous washes,

two in the day and two in the night,

they went to temples to worship the gods.

In the temples, during religious services, some priests wore white linen dresses with white sandals;

the other clothes had distinctive markings to indicate their location.

In fact, the priest who conducted the rite had a sash on his chest.

They didn't have to eat much and above all they didn't have to eat pork and fish to stay pure.

To be purer they had to shave their heads and bodies.

The high priest had the task of opening the sanctuary, washing the statue of the divinity,

dress her and perfume her.

Bowing before it, he sprinkled it with incense and recited hymns of worship.

The statue was served a real lunch, which was not consumed,

but made to burn by a fire.

Finally, the high priest sealed the door again and,

after having erased the traces of his footsteps, he withdrew.

The path from the entrance to the temple sanctuary

was seen as a journey from the human world to the divine realm,

Between the outer wall and the temple stood many

subsidiary buildings,

including workshops and storage areas to meet the needs of the temple,

and the library where the sacred writings and documents were kept,

and which also served as a study center for many disciplines.

The temple staff also included many other people,

beyond the priests, as musicians and singers of temple ceremonies.

Outside the temple there were craftsmen

and other workers who

contributed to its needs,

as well as the peasants who worked on Templar properties.

All were paid with portions of temple income.

The great temples were therefore important centers of economic activity,

sometimes with thousands of employees.

In the temple there were also functions related to the economic administration of the sanctuaries.

The priests had different tasks according to their seniority in the service.

During the Ancient and

Middle Kingdoms, there was no separate class of priests;
it was some government officials who assumed that role
for several months a year before returning to their usual duties.
Only in the New Kingdom did the "professional" priesthood spread,
although officials continued to exercise it for some time.
All were still civil servants and the pharaoh had the last word on them.
However, as the wealth of the temples grew, the influence of the priests increased,

until it rivaled that of the pharaoh.

In the political fragmentation of the Third Intermediate Period (about 1070 - 664 BC), the high priests of Amun at Karnak also became

the actual governors of Upper Egypt.

There were two types of temples: the temples of worship dedicated to a God,

the funerary temples which were built near the pyramids

The Egyptians believed that after death every man must pass through 12 underground kingdoms,

where various monsters who feared and escaped the light lived.

Exceeded these kingdoms, the dead came before a court,

whose leader was Osiris himself, who held the insignia of power,

that is a whip, symbol of punishment for the wicked,

and the stick of long life, a symbol of reward for good people.

Before Osiris, the deceased had to affirm that he had not committed bad deeds.

Then Anubis, assisted by Horus and Maat, the goddess of truth,

his heart weighed on a large scale.

The heart was considered the seat of feelings, will and

intelligence.

A feather was placed on the other side of the scale.

If the heart, burdened with too many faults, tipped the scales,

the deceased was devoured by the goddess Ammit, and condemned to be annihilated for eternity.

CHAPTER 3

THE HEROGLIFICES OF
ANCIENT EGYPT

Example of Egyptian hieroglyphs

The scriptures of ancient Egypt.

In Egypt, around 3,500 BC, a series of figures or hieroglyphs were adopted as writing, which were used both as ideograms and as phonograms.

The signs of this writing can be divided into:

- Pure ideograms;
- Phonograms, also used as ideograms;
- Phonograms indicating several consonants;
- Phonograms indicating a single consonant;
- Determinatives, ie ideograms which, when combined with homophonic words, specify their meaning;
- Phonetic complements: that is, mono-consonant phonograms that repeat some

or all of the consonants of a polyconsonant, or that express the phonetic value of an ideogram.

Egyptian writing subsequently developed into three types: hieroglyphic, hieratic, demotic:

- hieroglyphic: original writing carved on stone, later also used on papyrus for religious texts. The hieroglyphs are drawn very clearly and are arranged in columns from top to bottom or in lines. Both the columns and the lines run from right to left or vice versa; they look, ie they are open towards the beginning of the line, contrary to what happens in our writing;

- Hieratic: it is the cursive form of hieroglyphic writing, used simultaneously with it, but exclusively on papyrus. Until the New Kingdom, the particular signs are arranged in a column and from top to bottom; later they were arranged in lines. Both the columns and the lines go from right to left;

- demotic: it is a particular cursive that was used in the Low Epoch, without completely supplanting the hieratic script. The signs are arranged in lines from right to left.

From the Egyptian writing only the Meroitic writing is derived.

Hieroglyphics characters represent recognizable objects. The term hieroglyph is approached to the writing system of the ancient Egyptian language, but not only, because this word was later used to describe the pictorial writing systems developed by the Hittites, the Minoan civilization and the Maya.

Egyptian inscriptions are composed of two basic types of signs: ideograms and phonograms. The first indicates the object represented or something directly associated; the second represents sounds, and they are used for phonetic work.

Most of the words were written with a combination of phonetic and ideographic signs; for example, the representation of the plan of a house meant "home", but the same sign followed by a phonetic complement and the representation of a pair of legs in the act of walking was used to indicate the homophone verb which meant "to go out".

Generally, hieroglyphic inscriptions can have both horizontal and vertical trends and are read from right to left. In the sentences were found nouns, verbs, prepositions and other parts of speech arranged according to strict rules of word order. The hieroglyphic system developed around 3000 BC. and it was used by the Egyptians until Roman times;

the shape and number of signs remained unchanged until the Greco-Roman period.

Clay tablet with hieratic writing. Royal Ontario Museum, Toronto.

In religious hieratic writing text was used, cursive writing, spreading the ink with brushes on the papyrus.

In daily use, demotic writing was used, the drafting of which required accuracy, taking up double the time; it was used for inscriptions engraved on monuments.

These are the twenty-six one-letter signs that the Egyptians used most frequently to transcribe the sounds of their language.

Under each sign is the conventional name of the image and, in red, its pronunciation, although this does not exactly correspond to the Italian one.

For example, the W of the chick should be read "in English" as a U.

The forearm C is a sound halfway between the aspirated H and the A.

The courtyard H should be pronounced aspirated.

The H of twisted thread is a pharyngeal H.

The H in the basket resembles the German "ich".

The S of latch is sweet as in "isotope".

The cloth S is as harsh as the

"sun".

The S of the lake is pronounced like the Sc of "ski".

The Q in hill is a hard C, as in "flesh".

The K of cesta is a "Tuscan style" aspirated C.

The T of tethers is pronounced with a sound halfway between the T and the C.

The D of cobra stands between the D and G "people".

Statue of a scribe found in
Sakkara - 2,400 BC

Hieratic writing is the form
of Ancient Egyptian writing
currently used by scribes.
Developed together with or
following the so-called

hieroglyphic form (often for simplification), it was more suitable to be traced with a brush on papyrus and also on ostraka (stone).

Each glyph of the monumental (hieroglyphic) writing corresponds to a hieratic sign to the point that in the modern practice of Egyptology the texts in hieratic are often rendered in hieroglyphics.

The name, which means sacred writing, is of Greek origin and transmitted the incorrect conception that it was a form used only by priests.

From the hieratic was then derived the demotic, a simplified form of writing that came into use only in the first millennium BC.

ETYMOLOGY

Ιερογλυφικα γραμματαἶ
Ιερος - γλύφω - γραμμα
Sacred - engrave - letter
Engraved sacred letters
Ιερογλυφικός (= each of the signs of the pictographic script) Nieroglyïphcus (late Latin)
Hieroglyph (Old Italian).

PICTOGRAPHY

It is a form of writing in which each pictogram represented an object or element in a simplified way (papyrus, pyramid, etc.).

It could also correspond to a sound when it was necessary to write, for example, the name of a pharaoh or a city. Therefore each pictogram had both an ideographic and phonetic function used to decorate the temples.

IERATIC WRITING

The hieratic is the cursive development of hieroglyphic writing. It was used especially for the speed of writing for documents concerning public and religious life: therefore texts, novels, musical scores, medical prescriptions, private letters, diplomatic reports, etc ...

It appears during the III dynasty and it is used regularly until the end of the New Kingdom. In late times, the hieratic was used a lot in the religious field and was therefore called "ieratikos", that is, the priestly language.

DEMOTIC SCRUCTURE

The demotic originated around the 16th dynasty and is a simplification of the hieratic, in this case whole groups of words appearing with a single sign are shortened. This script was used extensively for the next thousand years.

The term demotic refers to the written language that translated the spoken language in use since the 15th dynasty. It is considered the popular language and was the favorite writing of legal scribes. It is much more difficult to read than the hieroglyph and the hieratic.

COPT WRITING

This script is the transcription of Egyptian into Greek elaborated by Egyptian Christians. It was adopted to replace the lack of vowels in the Egyptian alphabet.

It was used to write documents that allowed us to reconstruct a picture of post-pharaonic Egypt.

Chapter 4

THE ADORATION OF THE SUN - RA

One of the greatest and most ancient divinities present in the Egyptian pantheon is the figure of Ra, the supreme god of the sun depicted as a man with a hawk's head on whose top a solar disk persists. It became one of the main sacred figures of Egypt starting from the fifth dynasty around 2510 BC. - 2350 BC This happened thanks above all to the expansion of the power of the priestly caste in the inviolable city of Heliopolis (Ἡλίου πόλις- Heliopolis in Greek: City of the Sun).

The god ruled over the whole of reality, regardless of whether it was heaven, earth or the world of the dead; and it was the manifestation of the primordial celestial and demiurge power for humanity.

There are several evolutions of the figure of him over the centuries; he was often compared to the god Horus with whom he was merged creating the god Ra-Horakhty.

Ra-Horakhty carved in the center of the facade of the main temple of Abu-Simbel, while being worshiped by Ramesses II.

This new eternal being was nothing but a kind of renewed Ra, lord of the Two Horizons. Basically a sun that would never have seen a sunset and would never end. Subsequently, the solar god was joined to the Theban Amon in the period of the XII dynasty (1994 BC - 1794 BC), giving rise to one of the most important deities of the entire pantheon: Amon-Ra, king of all gods.

A brief parenthesis occurred in the dominion of Ra exclusively during the domination of Amenhotep IV from about 1351 BC. to 1334

BC The Pharaoh decided to suppress the cult of the great Amon to make room for the adoration of a new solar entity: the Aten. The symbol par excellence of this divinity was the solar disc which generally dominated the sovereign, granting him the benevolence of him. A presence, that of Aten, vivifying and active.

So great was the change of direction that Pharaoh himself changed his name from Amenhotep (literally: Amon is satisfied) in Akhenaten (Horizon of Aten). Indeed such was at a certain point the dominance imposed by Aten that many scholars believe this phenomenon to be an ancient precursor of the first monotheisms, that is a real enotheism (from the ancient Greek εἷς "one" and θεός "god", a term coined by Max Müller , indicates a type of religiosity that foresees the pre-eminence of a god over all the others, such as to center all worship on it). For example, early Judaism is also believed to be very close to enotheism, starting from the Canaanite pantheon (of the land of Canaan) with the main god El and then reaching El Shaddai in mature age, one of the numerous names with which it was defined Yahweh. But let's go back to Akhenaten. Due to the various conflicts that arose between the royal family and the priestly caste for this new cult which tended to exclude many of the most ancient and traditional gods of the Egyptian pantheon, there is no clear information on the fate of the pharaoh.

The only certainty is that he was condemned to damnatio memoriae (Latin phrase which literally means condemnation of memory. In Roman law it indicated a penalty consisting in the cancellation of a person's memory and in the destruction of any trace that could pass it on to posterity(as if it were never existed), with consequent destruction of all documents, cartouches and monuments that represented it. We also know that he was succeeded by his son Tutankhamun, who, as his name suggests, restored the cult of Amon and all the other deities with immediate effect.

Ra, which was the sun at midday, at the height of its splendor, was therefore for the

Egyptians a symbol of light, warmth and prosperity. Presence inseparable from what should have been the life of any inhabitant of Ancient Egypt. It marked the rhythm of the days, invigorated the crops, allowed the carrying out of a thousand and more activities. And, although darkness came, he always made his eternal return, regardless of how dark the night might have been.

The importance of the shining diurnal star was such that other minor solar deities descended from it such as: Atum, god of the setting sun;

Khepri, god of the rising sun; Sekhmet, goddess of war, depicted as a lioness-headed woman with a solar globe on her head symbolizing the deadly heat of the sun's rays; Harmakis, god of the dawn and dusk sun that we also find depicted in the sphinx of Giza.

The origin of Ra is lost in myth, there are different cosmogonies inherent in his birth, his advent and the power he exercised. Much depended on the beliefs of the priestly order under consideration. For example, the priests of the city of Heliopolis believed that Ra first created himself, self-generating, from what were the waters of the primordial ocean Nun, then transported between the horns of the celestial heifer Mehetueret and finally forged the world. Instead the followers of Ptah, an ancient creator and demiurgic god, fundamental for the city of Memphis, believed that Ra himself had been shaped by the will of this supreme body patron of knowledge and knowledge, and only later the star would be found to play such a prominent role in the Egyptian pantheon.

According to the most accredited belief, it was always Ra who gave rise to men through his tears. Through the blood of him, self-imposed, circumcision would have given life to the goddesses Sia and Hu, the first personification of perception and the second instead of command. As already mentioned, Ra was also the organizer of all things, from the seasons to plants and animals. His benevolence for the Egyptians, who regulated everything that belonged to both worlds (the earthly and the afterlife) was of incalculable value, based precisely on his constant presence and guidance. It is no coincidence that the people of the Nile believed that the king of the gods travelled on two sacred solar boats: the first called Mandjet, the morning boat; the second was called Mesektet, the evening boat. These two means of transportation had the task of leading Ra through Heaven and the Duat, the realm of the dead. When the god was on the night boat with which he travelled the afterlife, he changed, and his falcon head became that of a ram, while maintaining the distinctive sign of the solar disc between the horns. The Eternal in this nocturnal journey was escorted, at times, by several minor deities, including Sia, Hu and Bastet (warrior goddess) and other gods of the Enneade (group of nine gods that are the basis of the Egyptian cosmogony) who they had the task of supporting him in the fight against the primordial serpent of chaos Apopi. The latter in fact constantly tried to interrupt the journey of Ra's boat to prevent the return of light with the new day. This continuous pilgrimage between the two extremes of the day was nothing more than the symbolic attempt to explain, with the instrument of the etiological myth, the rising and setting of the Sun, placing a clear emphasis on the divine qualities necessary to accomplish this type of undertaking. Only the supreme god Ra could be able to face such an uncertain and difficult journey to be able to return to shine in the celestial vault, granting his favor to the adoring populations in the lands of the great Nile.

As we have already seen, many interpretations and beliefs regarding the origin, the area of competence of the deities and their role within the Egyptian pantheon depended heavily on the dominant priestly order in their respective cities. Precisely for the aforementioned reasons, the classification of the god Horus is not easy to elaborate. He was born in turn as one of the most remote eternals present in the cosmogonies of ancient Egypt. The iconography saw him represented as a hawk, sometimes even in anthropomorphic form. The main seat of his cult was the city of Edfu. Despite this primacy of celestial antiquity, the priestly caste of Eliopoli soon tried to undermine its foundations by placing the figure of their god Ra in direct competition with him; reaching the almost total assimilation of it, through the fusion of both in the aforementioned figure of Ra-Horakhty, the Ra-Horus of the Two Horizons (sunrise and sunset). This also had repercussions on the representation of this new entity, leading to the portrait that often emerges in the collective imagination of a hawk-headed man with a head crowned with a solar disc.

The most accredited theories want to see in this final result an attempt by the priestly class to reach a satisfactory compromise for all.

In any case, with the succession of the different ruling dynasties, it was deemed appropriate to split the two entities again. This time Horus came to assume the role of the son of Osiris and Isis. He was the god of death and ruler of the underworld and she was the goddess of magic and fertility. This latest reworking would have involved the inclusion of the falcon god as the definitive avenger of the murder of his father by the god of chaos Seth. The latter was none other than the brother of Osiris himself.

The saga that arose would become one of the most relevant in the great divine complex of the Egyptian universe.

As we have been able to understand, even an ancient cosmogony such as the

Egyptian one is subject to the fleeting changes of human history. The same divinities that with laudable abundance they tried to make immutable and granite in their eternal glory, came to assume different forms and different roles to reconcile the need for the illusory human order. But even more important is how much man, an inhabitant of the banks of the Nile, saw in the bright star of every day such a profound meaning combined with such a great awareness of the fragility of life in his time. A man who, despite the innumerable difficulties, chose to devote himself to the grace of light, rather than to the unknown of darkness.

Statue of Horus (Temple of Edfu,   modern day Egypt)

Chapter 5

THE BURIAL RITUALS IN ANCIENT EGYPT

WORSHIP OF THE DEAD

The Egyptians believed that man was born with two souls: the Ba and the Ka.

The Ba was destined to make the journey to the afterlife,

where he received the reward or punishment that was due to her;

the Ka was meant to remain with the body

and to keep him in the grave. as long as the provisions lasted.

The Egyptians, in fact, thought that after death there was another life;

for this reason they mummified the bodies of the pharaohs to allow the dead

to keep the body for a long time in the afterlife

and thus allowed it to survive.

In the tombs they placed food, clothing and cosmetics, portraits of the deceased,

and a kind of stone casket engraved with a door

to allow the deceased to go from the world of the living to that of the dead.

Living in the afterlife was simple and it was easy:

the Egyptians believed that life in the afterlife took place in a kind of rural paradise,

in the papyrus fields, ruled by the god Osiris.

They thought that after death, the soul, after having remained for some time in the grave,

came out and went before the god Osiris.

If the opinion of this god was favorable, the soul could enter the bean fields,

who are of inexhaustible fertility where the dead could work and,

when they were tired they could be replaced by their "respondents"

that is, statuettes that were placed in their graves for this purpose.

Before reaching eternal life,
however, the deceased had to
defeat the monsters
    and cross the lakes of fire;
but if he had the book of the
dead
    which contained the prayers
to exorcise them, the obstacles

were easily overcome.

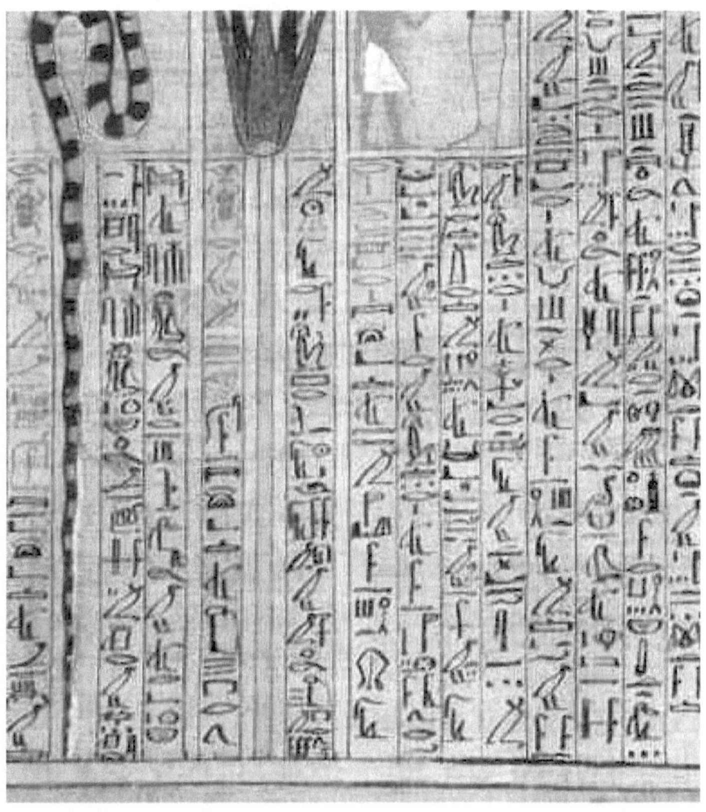

The hardest test to pass was the last one:

Anubis carried the dead to Osiris and his 42 judges,

weighing the heart of the dead with the feather of the Goddess Maat.

If the heart weighed more than the feather, the deceased was devoured by Ammut, a terrifying monster,

if the heart weighed like the feather it went towards eternal life.

According to the Egyptians, the soul was equal to the body and therefore, when a child was born, his double or Kâ was also born

who faithfully followed the individual until death.

He was sitting next to the
mummy when the man died
while the food lasted
    which it was customary to
deposit in the grave,
    then, beset by hunger, he
went out in search of food.

In the excavations, archaeologists have discovered the tools that the ancient Egyptians used to mummify corpses:

they had various shapes and were used to extract the internal organs from the body of the dead.

Only a few knew the art of mummification;

assigned to this task were the embalmers.

When a dead man was brought to them, they would show relatives wooden models in the shape of a man,

painted in natural colors and asked how they wanted the dead to be treated.

Once the price was agreed upon, the embalmers began work.

The mummification process, which lasted months, was preceded by a beer-based wash, evident symbol of purification for the sacral character and for the divine origin of the drink.

Therefore, they extracted all

the organs, except the heart which in the afterlife had to be weighed.

The brain was extracted from the nose with a hook.

Subsequently the corpse was made with a sharp stone a cut on the abdomen

through which the vital organs were removed and dried with salt,

treated with oils and resins and then placed in containers called canopic jars

which were placed near the sarcophagus.

Each jar had a lid with the face of a god and was painted with ritual formulas to protect the organs.

After cleaning the cavity with palm wine, and filling it with myrrh, cinnamon and other perfumed essences,

straw and rags, they stitched up the abdomen with needle and thread

The body was left for 40 days in a saline compound called natron

to make the body give up all fluids;

Natron was nothing but sodium carbonate hydrate which stopped rot

Its name derives from the Egyptian word for salt "Ntry", which means pure.

The substance gave its name to the ancient quarry, Wadi el-Natrun,

a nearly dry lake in Egypt that contained high amounts of sodium carbonate.

At the end it was washed with a ceremony in the waters of the Nile to remove the residual salt.

Immediately afterwards it was left to dry for 20 days.

Then the dry skin was softened by massaging it and spreading it with oils and resins too.

After this procedure the body was wrapped in several layers

of bandages cut from a linen sheet.

Sometimes the bandages were smeared with resins and ointments that were intended to seal and perfume.

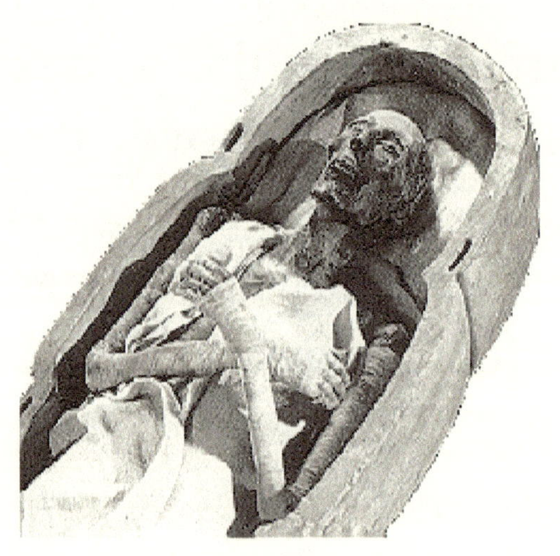

The mummies could have more than twenty layers of bandages and in the various layers,

amulets, jewels and gold necklaces were placed on the chest of the deceased

to protect the heart which was a symbol of life

and to protect the deceased against evil or to give him strength;

The BEETLE symbolized the resurrection and was placed on or inside the chest

It was shaped like a dung beetle and was chosen

because they believed it was able to spontaneously regenerate itself from its own excrement.

The DJED column conferred stability and firmness and symbolized the backbone of

Osiris.

The most powerful amulet, however, was the Eye of Horus or WEDJET health giver.

Then the deceased was placed inside a man-shaped coffin. The mummification process lasted a total of 70 days.

It must be said that in the Book of the Dead in the chapter dealing with embalming in the House of the Dead,

it is specified that only the Pharaohs, dignitaries, priests and the most important personalities of the kingdom,

they were entitled to this treatment which, by preserving the body, ensured the immortality of the soul.

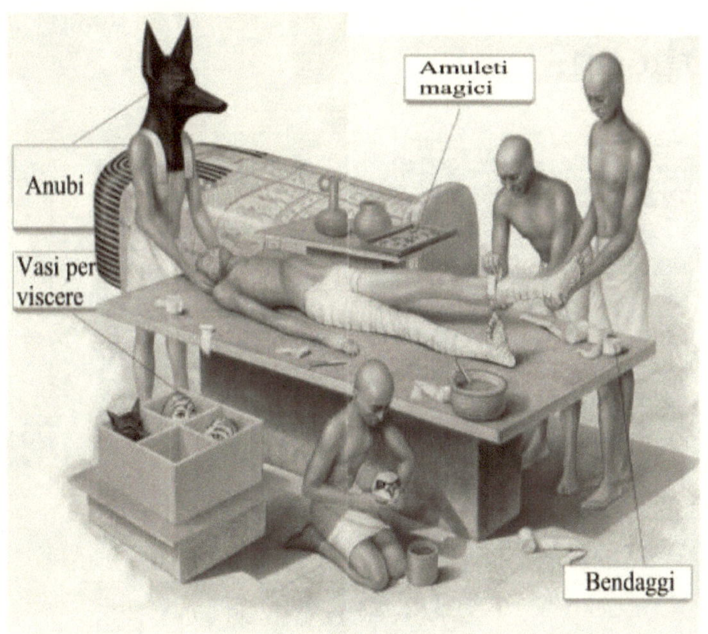

Only these characters were the custodians, by divine will, of a soul that became part of the afterlife

and only the Pharaohs, after death, became divinities, occupying a precise place in the complicated Egyptian pantheon.

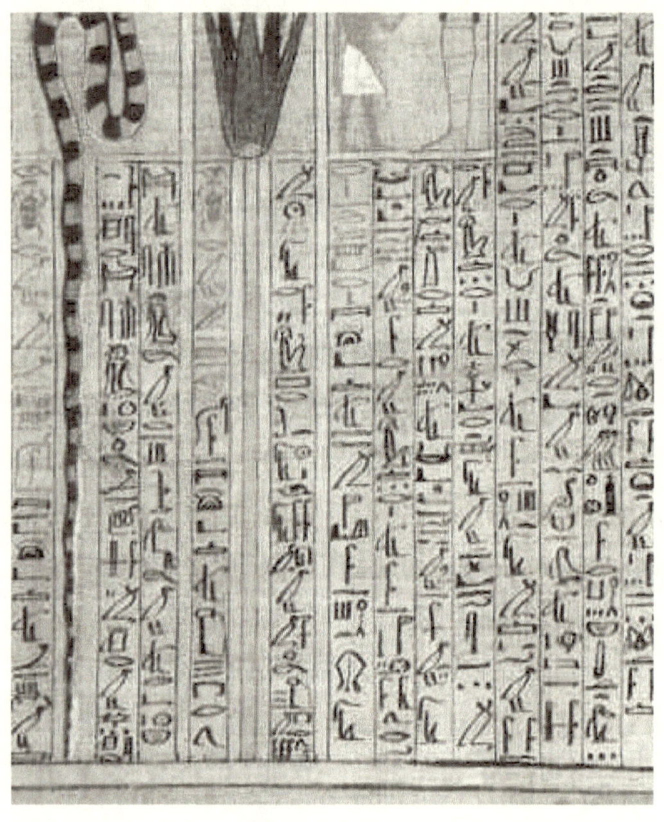

In a text from the Old Kingdom, preserved in the Sakkara pyramids, to the description of what was needed by the deceased for the long journey beyond the grave,

always appears the hieroglyph of zythum and curmy. that is beer:

"zythum" was the light beer, "curmy" the darker colored beer,

During the endless and exhausting funeral ceremonies, all present

to honor the deceased they made abundant libations of beer,

as we read on the papyrus of Prisse found in the necropolis

of Abido

and who advised: "You will not let the pain take you to the point of numbing yourself,

but you will find solace by drinking zythum and curmy ...."

(from papyri preserved in the Egyptian museum in Turin). The priests completed the funeral service by drinking sa,

(high concentration beer, reserved for the exclusive consumption of the Pharaoh and for religious ceremonies)

as they intoned the funeral lament which roughly said:

"It's sad to get on Rie's boat

with no hope of finding plenty of zythum and curmy as your soul would like ...."

Ramses III (1300 BC) boasted of having donated 463,000 jars of beer to the powerful deity Ishtar throughout his life.

The goddess of fertility, love, but also protector of sailors and armies,

as her litany goes:
"Morning star
star of the sea
queen of the earth
patroness of sailors

leader of the armies "

Ishtar was identified on the planet Venus, the first and brightest star to appear in the night sky.

In her honor the temple of

Medinet-Habu had been erected where, with meticulous meticulousness,

the foodstuffs taken were noted in the accounting tablets,

and the daily consumption of drinks: 144 skins of beer, and some of wine and date wine.

This proves, if there is still a need, besides the sacredness of this drink,

also its proportions of consumption compared to the others.

After the mummification, her body was placed in a sarcophagus.

A death mask was placed on

the mummy's head

made in likeness to the deceased precisely to help the spirit recognize its own body.

Then the sarcophagus was placed in the tomb, in which they were also placed,

the grave goods of the deceased: clothes, ornaments, objects of use and, at the same time, a supply of food and drink,

that were to serve the soul in her new life.

In the grave goods of the deceased there were beds and pillows:

as well as for rest in earthly

life, they also served in the afterlife.

In reliefs and tomb paintings, pillows used for sleeping were often depicted as they were in reality: above the beds.

The ancient Egyptians gave more importance to tombs than to dwelling houses because, always according to the belief, they would have lived longer in the tomb.

For this reason the tombs were particularly well cared for, and built with more resistant materials.

Over time, different types of tombs were used:

while the poor were buried in modest graves or even in the desert sand,

the rich were given the privilege of a majestic tomb.

Initially the nobles were buried in mastabas, masonry tombs in the shape of a truncated pyramid;

Subsequently for the pharaohs next to these tombs, others even more impressive were built:

the pyramids, gigantic funeral monuments that testified to the greatness of the person buried inside them.

The construction of these tombs took a lot of time and effort.

In addition to slaves, peasants also participated in their construction.

The latter collaborated in the work only in the period of flood of the Nile, when it was impossible to work in the fields.

Since treasures of great value were placed with the body in these tombs, they were often violated by thieves.

Then, the architects began to build underground type tombs,

digging them deep into the rocks

and masking from the outside , every element that could indicate its existence.

The greatest examples of these particular tombs can be seen in the Valley of the Kings and the Valley of the Queens, not far from Luxor.

As for the practices of funerals, they ranged from exposure to the late public

at the funeral procession at the banquet in front of the tomb.

In fact, at the funeral, relatives offered food and priests performed special rituals.

These ceremonies were to protect the deceased on his journey to the afterlife.

For added support, ritual

images and texts were placed on the body of the deceased or used to decorate the tomb.

The ritual of opening the mouth was performed before the burial,

since in this way the senses would be reactivated and the deceased could continue to live in the afterlife.

A description of the ritual came to us from the decorations of the tomb of Seti I (KV17 in the Valley of the Kings) ,

in whose corridors there are 75 panels illustrating the ceremony.

Another description comes from the famous tomb of Tutankhamen.

One of the ritual objects of the ceremony was
the golden finger, an object in gold, or painted stone,

depicting two fingers side by side

while the other was the nechereti, a small ax

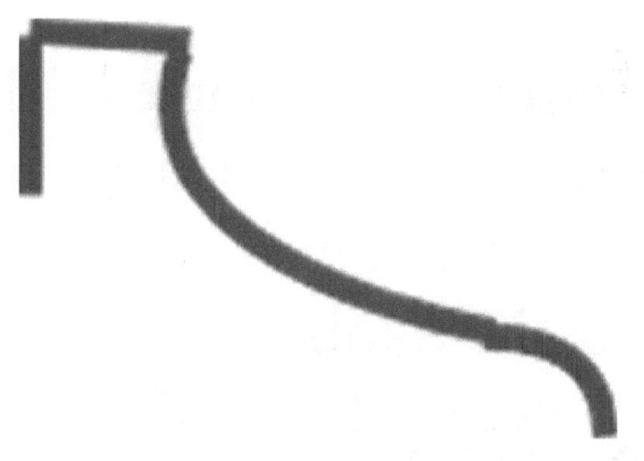

which is clearly seen in the hands of the priest on the right in the illustration.

.

The ceremony, in its earliest phase, took place in the sacred laboratory attached to the temple,

called the golden castle where the statue was made.

The ritual was completed by fumigations and lustrations that preceded the transport of the statue to the tomb.

In its later evolution the ritual was extended to the mummy

in order to restore the use of the senses so that the ka of the deceased

could live fully of the Duat (the afterlife).

This ceremony ensured the

deceased could eat, drink, talk and have sexual intercourse.

During its development, the dead man also regained his sight.

For the Egyptians (as well as in other cultures) " seeing " was synonymous with " living ".

Therefore, the full name of the ritual was `` opening ceremony of the mouth and eyes ".

After the funeral procession had arrived at the necropolis, the ritual was performed by the priests

and on the basis of the representations, we know that

it took place in front of the tomb of the deceased.

After placing the mummy or statue of the deceased on a mound of earth,

reminiscent of the primordial hill, a purification was performed

through a libation with water through the nemeset (a round jar) and

a sprinkling of incense or natron from Upper and Lower Egypt.

Then the funeral priest or sem performed the first rites of resurrection

and made the first gesture of

opening the mouth and eyes with the dyeba

with which he touched the mouth of the mummy or that of the statue)

and the nechereti with which he opened it.

The people did not have any kind of soul, despite the internal and external ablutions of beer, in life and in the dead.

All these practices, along with the ceremonies and rites that needed to be performed

in honor of divinities

connected with the funerary sphere, they were part of an authentic cult of the dead, sacred to respect and venerate.

However, the situation changed over time: in fact, due to suggestions from the Greek world,

during the 5th century BC, to the primitive belief in survival of the dead in the grave and

the idea of a special kingdom of the dead was replaced.

This was imagined on the model of the Greek Avernus (or Acheron), ruled by the divine couple of Aita and Phersipnai (Greek Hades and

Persephone).

IDEAS FOR MORE INFORMATION:

Greek mythology was and is the collection and therefore the study of Greek myths belonging to the religious culture of the ancient Greeks and concerning, in particular, their gods and heroes. The Greek myths were collected in cycles concerning the different areas of the Hellenic world. The only unifying element is the composition of the Greek pantheon, consisting of a hierarchy of divine figures that also represent the forces or aspects of nature. Contemporary scholars study and analyze ancient myths in an attempt to shed light on the political and religious institutions of ancient Greece and, in general, of all ancient Greek civilization. It consists of a large collection of tales explaining the origin of the world and detailing the life and adventures of a large number of gods and goddesses, heroes and heroines and other mythological creatures. These stories were initially composed and disseminated in an oral poetic and compositional form, while they have come down to us mainly through the texts written by the Greek literary tradition. The oldest known literary sources, the two epic poems Iliad and Odyssey, focus their attention on the events that revolve around the story of the Trojan War. Two other poems almost contemporary to the Homeric works, the Theogony and The works and days written by Hesiod, instead contain stories concerning the genesis of the world, the chronology of celestial rulers, the succession of the ages of man, the beginning of human suffering. and the origin of sacrificial practices. Several myths are also contained in the Homeric hymns, in the fragments of the poems of the epic cycle, in the poems of the Greek lyricists, in the works of the tragedians of the fifth century BC, in the writings of scholars and poets of the Hellenistic age and in writers such as Plutarch and Pausanias. The topics narrated by Greek mythology were also represented in many artifacts: the geometric designs on the surface of vases and plates dating back to the 8th century BC, they portray scenes inspired by the cycle of the Trojan War or by the adventures of Heracles. Even later, scenes from Homer or other myths will be represented on the art objects, in order to provide scholars with additional material to support the literary texts. It had a huge influence on the culture, arts and literature of Western civilization and its legacy is still very much alive in its languages and cultures. It has always been presented in the educational system, starting from the earliest degrees of education, while poets and artists of all eras have been inspired by it, highlighting the relevance and weight that classical mythological themes could play in all eras of history.

Thank you...
Thank you...
Thank you...